WALKS wi

in the Lake District
AROUND CONISTON

Ron Bickerton

A Questa Guide

© Ron Bickerton, 1994, 2000
ISBN 1 898808 20 1
Reprinted with revisions, 2000

ADVICE TO READERS

Readers are advised that while the author had made every effort to
ensure the accuracy of this guidebook, and has been required to
revisit all the routes during the course of preparing the book,
changes can occur which may affect the contents. The Publishers
would welcome notes of any changes you find.

Also by Ron Bickerton
Walks with Children in the Lake District:
Buttermere and the Vale of Lorton
Keswick and the Newlands Valley

Published by
Questa Publishing, 27 Camwood, Bamber Bridge, Preston, Lancashire
PR5 8LA
and printed by
Carnmor Print, 95/97 London Road, Preston, Lancashire

Contents

Introduction

The fells around Coniston are a small compact arrangement that contains many of the best and most endearing features of the Lake District. The high fells, composed of Borrowdale Volcanic Series rock, with rugged east-facing corries, form the southern frontier of Lakeland, giving way to the gentle folds of Silurian moorland interwoven with beautiful woodland valleys that not even the scars of long derelict industries can defile. To the east of the lake, oak and conifer mantle the fells of Monk Coniston Moor and Carron Crag, all former sheep walks and grazing grounds for Furness Abbey.

In *Days in Lakeland: Past and Present* written in 1929, E.M. Ward comments: "Here at Coniston there is not that triumphant, defiant splendour of scenery that is apt, as at Ullswater, to baffle the flow of easy description in even the most hardened writer. There is quietness at Coniston. The queer, sleepy little village is away from the lake, whose waters lie amidst low fells sufficiently monotonous in their aspect to give full value to every brightness and shadowing of the great sheet of water, and every stirring of wind and sunshine through the coppice woods upon its banks."

Coniston village is not so sleepy now, nor would I concede any monotony among its fells, save that of consistent ruggedness and grandeur. While those pre-occupied with industrial archaeology will find in and around Coniston a wealth of interest to fill many a day.

The village, of course, no longer relies on mining for its economy, but on tourism and boating. Serious tourism began with the opening of the Furness Railway in 1859, originally for the more efficient transportation of copper ore and slate to the coast. But this scenic ride, through wooded glades and rock cuttings, soon became popular with less industrious visitors, who came simply to view the beauties of the lake and the surrounding countryside. With the decline of the mines the line from Foxfield closed after almost 100 years of continuous operation.

Alas, no one was able to record for posterity the beginnings of Coniston. All the countryside was buried in woodland, quite remote from the gaze of unconcerned visitors. The early people of Coniston lived on the uplands, on the Monk Coniston moors, the Torver moors, the Blawiths, where even today you might still find evidence of their existence in garths and graves and hut circles.

Although the main, probably the only, attraction of the region around Coniston Water for the early settlers and the people of medieval times was its great cloak of forest - material for charcoal, buildings, tools and weapons - the natural beauty was the biggest attraction for the early tourists. Writing in *British Tourists* in 1797 a "Gentleman of Oxford" commented "The character of Coniston is romantic; and this character gives such scope for imagination, that where it prevails, the beauty of the landscape must be supreme."

Coniston, Wordsworth declared "May be conveniently visited from Ambleside, but is seen to most advantage by entering the country over the Sands from Lancaster. The Stranger, from the moment he sets his foot on those Sands, seems to leave the turmoil and traffic of the world behind him; and...he beholds...the cluster of mountains among which he is going to wander, and towards whose recesses, by the Vale of Coniston, he is gradually and peacefully led." You can still make this approach, and experience all the feelings Wordsworth describes, though shifting channels in the Kent Estuary have ensured that a crossing of Morecambe Bay from Lancaster is a thing of the past for all but the most experienced. Today, you must expect to cross from Arnside, though you face a mighty trail to reach Coniston.

In 1127 Stephen, later King Stephen, gave the whole of Furness, except the lands belonging to Michael le Fleming, to a colony of monks from the Norman-French abbey of Savigny. In 1148 the parent abbey joined the Cistercian order, but not so the distant colony in Furness, whose abbot, Peter of York, appealed to the Pope to sanction its freedom. On his way home, Peter, was seized by Savigny monks and, according to the official record, heavy with meaning, "resigned his office as abbot, and became a most worthy monk...learning the Cistercian Order". In similar vein, Savigny sent a Frenchman to Furness, "by whose diligence and counsel" the abbey at Furness succumbed to the new Order.

Furness Abbey owned massive blocks of land, including the greater part of High and Low Furness together with many extensive sheep pastures, notably in upper Eskdale and Borrowdale. Their empire even reached as far as the Isle of Man and into Ireland and Yorkshire. The role of the Abbey in shaping the landscape we see today is most evident around Coniston, large tracts of which were once cloaked in forest, but were denuded for the production of charcoal to fire the bloomeries required by the copper mines, and to provide grazing for sheep.

Coniston Water, known originally as Thurstane Watter, used to be an important fishery for Furness Abbey, and the monks had the right to keep a boat and twenty nets on the lake. Today, the lake is largely associated with the names of Sir Malcolm and Donald Campbell, who used the lake for their world water speed records. Donald met his death on Coniston Water in 1967, and still lies in the depths of the lake along with his boat, *Bluebird*.

But Coniston was not all industry; it had its literary connections, too. Wordsworth went to school nearby at Hawkshead, and in later life made many visits to Coniston. Alfred Tennyson (1809-1892), who succeeded Wordsworth as poet laureate in 1850, spent his honeymoon at Tent Lodge on the east shore of the lake. While at Brantwood, Eliza Lynn Linton, the novelist, and her poet and engraver husband William James lived until their separation in 1867. The house was later sold to John Ruskin in 1871, who lived there until his death in 1900. In more recent times, Arthur Ransome used the setting of Coniston Water and the Old Man of Coniston for his tales *Swallows and Amazons* and *Swallowdale*.

1

Yew Tree Tarn

This is a brief, easy and interesting walk on which to introduce young family members to country walking. Progress around the tarn is enlivened by bright yellow expanses of marsh marigolds and flag irises along the wet ground between the tree-lined path and the water's edge. The reeds along the tarn shore provide excellent cover for coots, moorhen and mallard, while visitors early in the day may be rewarded with a glimpse of the families of greylag geese that frequent this tiny tarn. If you choose a spring day and an early start you are sure to see Yew Tree Tarn at its best.

Start: Layby on A593. GR322003
Total distance: 1km (½ mile)
Height gain: 10m (30 feet)
Difficulty: Easy walking on well-defined path, but with a few unbridged streams to cross

1   Leave the layby at the southern (Coniston) end on a path that takes you to a dam at the outflow of the tarn. Cross the dam and a wooden bridge over the sluice, and then a simple, unguarded bridge. Continue for about 200m/yds before crossing a small stream.

2   Follow the path through trees to a step stile, shortly after which another stream is crossed by stepping stones. *[Take care with very young children here.]*

3   To avoid wet ground, now turn left and follow the stream to a wall junction, and here turn right and head for a wooden bridge (not immediately visible) on a grassy path through larch trees.

4   Cross the bridge, and walk along the ensuing farm track to a

field gate in a wall. Don't go through the gate, but turn right alongside the wall and cross a wire fence by a step stile. If you now follow the wall it will lead you back to the layby at which you started.

- ***Yew Tree Tarn:***
- *During the nineteenth century James Marshall of Monk*
- *Coniston built a dam at the southern end of a former moss to*
- *create Yew Tree Tarn. To the northern end a large rectangle*
- *with a water feed from the beck was constructed for fish*
- *breeding, and to keep the tarn stocked.*
- *Against a backdrop of plantations of larch and oak this*
- *artificial tarn now blends well with its surroundings, and is now*
- *in the care of the National Trust.*

Juniper scrub

Locally known as 'savin', thickets of juniper are a characteristic Lakeland vegetation type, both on the uplands and the lower fells. The high level scrub is thought to exist on the sites of former forests.
Juniper does not tolerate shading by trees, so where oaks and birches have grown to maturity you find that the juniper has become moribund. An example of this can be seen in the woodland, not far from Yew Tree Tarn, on the south side of Oxenfell, east of the Coniston-Ambleside road.

2

Tarn Hows
and Tarn Hows Cottage

*Tarn Hows, one time water and power supply to a saw
mill, was landscaped and planted by James Marshall of
Monk Coniston, creating a picturesque foreground to
views of the Helvellyn range and the Langdale Pikes.
This walk from the head of Coniston Water passes
through delightful woodland planted with large pines from
North America, and returns by way of Tarn Hows
Cottage, pleasantly enclosed by larch trees, and along
an old pony track once used to carry slate and copper
ore from Tilberthwaite to Kirby Quay on Coniston Water.*

Start: Water Head car park. GR316978
Total distance: 8km (5 miles)
Height gain: 280m (920 feet)
Difficulty: This is an agreeable and quiet walk on well-
maintained paths and tracks, along which the route-
finding is easy.

1   From the car park take the road left along the head of the lake
to a road junction. Cross the road to a gate through which you turn
right (northeast) along a fenced path beside the road, to rejoin the
road at Boon Crag Cottage.

2   Turn left in front of the cottage, cross a side road, and pass in
front of the next cottage to a wicket gate on your left, giving into a
field. Keep to the fence on your right, then leave it, left, to a gate
to the road.

3   Cross the road to a bridleway (signposted: Tarn Hows), and
follow this as it climbs steadily through pine trees.

4   The track passes a series of pools well-stocked with yellow iris,

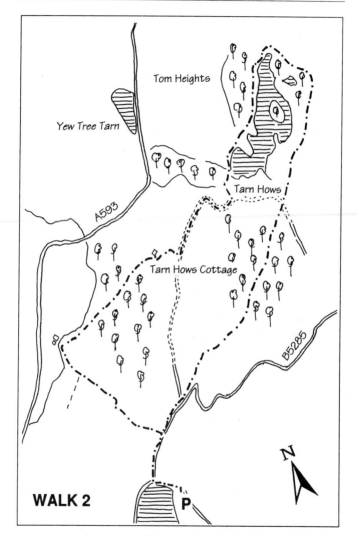

Tom Heights

Yew Tree Tarn

A593

Tarn Hows

Tarn Hows Cottage

B5285

N

WALK 2   P

and continues through a gap in a wall – to your right a small dam creates a long narrow pool favoured by dragon- and damsel-flies. Soon the track levels, and you cross a beck, continuing past diverging tracks, right and left, to reach a fork. Here, branch right on an ascending track (signposted: Tarn Hows old car park) that soon narrows and climbs beside a wall. Shortly, turn left on to a broad track and follow the wall to a road.

5   Cross the road, pass through an area set aside for disabled parking to reach a broad track descending northeast towards Tarn Hows. At a cross track, turn right onto a broad well-made track which will take you round the tarn by a wooded walk to a dam and gate.

- ***Tarn Hows***
- *Tarn Hows is not the name of the tarn at all. Strictly, the tarn*
- *has no name, being no more than an artificial pond created by*
- *damming a stream and a few pools of marshland. The name*
- *applies not to the tarn, but to the hill above it; it is not, as is*
- *usually supposed, the 'tarn beside the hill', but the 'hill beside*
- *the tarn'.*
- *Tarn Hows is now in the care of the National Trust, founded*
- *in 1895 by the crusading work of Canon Rawnsley, vicar of*
- *Wray and of Crosthwaite, near Keswick. In the early days,*
- *Rawnsley's chief concern was the threat to the Lake District*
- *posed by the developers of housing estates and railway.*
- *Tarn Hows was bought by Beatrix Potter, better known*
- *locally as Mrs William Heelis. She sold half at cost to the Trust*
- *(the purchase being funded by Sir Samuel Scott), and*
- *bequeathed to it the other half.*
- *The Trust has created a new section of path around the*
- *tarns to enable those with walking difficulties to enjoy the place,*
- *but there are unavoidably some steep inclines that could cause*
- *problems for visitors in wheelchairs without the company of*
- *strong helpers.*

6   Go through the gate and take an ascending track towards the road, there turning right to follow the road past a car park. Then go on for about 700m/yds to a track on your right. Signposted 'Yewdale', the track runs between a wall on the left and mature oak and rowan trees to the right before reaching a gate into the grounds of Tarn Hows Cottage.

7   A signpost directs you left to Low Yewdale and Coniston along a path through two gates, after which you turn right on a broad, descending path, keeping ahead through trees to the banks of Yewdale Beck.

8   Turn left alongside the beck, cross a fence by a stile, and keep a new hedge on your right as you make for a gate and a bridge near a large tree.

9   Do not cross the beck, but go through a gate and turn left on a track, first beside the beck and then climbing between walls and fences before descending to Boon Crag Farm.

10 Stay on the track through the farm buildings and continue to the road ahead. Turn right, pass Boon Crag Cottage once more to a gated footpath beside the road. Use the footpath to the first gate on the left, at a road junction, where you leave the path and cross to the road opposite, following this back to the car park at Water Head.

- **Boon Crag Farm and cottage**
- *Formerly part of the Monk Coniston Estate, and purchased by*
- *Beatrix Potter in 1930, the farm is still active, while the cottage*
- *and its outbuildings are a maintenance depot for the work of the*
- *National Trust.*

The Arrival of Spring
One of the surest signs that spring is on the way is the sound of curlews on the air. These delightful moorland birds start to arrive in the Lake District towards the end of February, often at the same time as lesser black backed gulls. Reed buntings return to the nesting places in March, or earlier, while around the shores of lakes and tarns, and well up the fells, along the becks and tarns, you will see and hear the common sandpiper. Kingfishers re-appear, too, but these are difficult to spot, often glimpsed only briefly as a darting flash of iridescent blue - a breathtaking moment when you do see it.

3

Tom Heights and Hodge Close

*This outstanding walk starts by ascending through
peaceful oak woodland, along the course of Tom Gill
with its cascading beck and attractive waterfalls, and
leads to Tarn Hows. With only a brief halt at this popular
spot, the walk goes on to explore the volcanic outcrops
that adorn Tom Heights, which provide remarkable views
of Coniston Water and the broad sweep of the Lakeland
fells from the Old Man of Coniston to the long, undulating
line of the Helvellyn and Fairfield massifs.
Hodge Close is renowned for the high quality of its
green-hued slate, which it supplied to the world.*

Start: Glen Mary Bridge. GR322999
Total distance: 8km (5 miles)
Height gain: 360m (1,180 feet)
Difficulty: Pleasant walk through wooded glens, along
narrow country lanes and across the craggy undulating
top of Tom Heights.
Children will need careful supervision in the vicinity of
Hodge Close, where the quarry waters are over 30m
(100ft) deep, and have very steep sides.

1 From the parking area cross Tom Gill by a wooden bridge and
ascend its left (true right) bank, passing cascades and a delightful
waterfall, to reach the dam of Tarn Hows.

- *Monk Coniston Estate*
- Formerly owned by James Marshall, a noted geologist who
- studied the metamorphic rocks of this area. The Marshalls
- were responsible for damming many small tarns on the estate
- to provide fishing for guests. The estate was purchased in
- 1930 by Beatrix Potter, and is now in the ownership of the
- National Trust.

2   Turn left along a well-made track circling the tarn. Shortly after you pass a seat, go left on a path climbing through rowan and silver birch and across bracken-clad slopes to reach the rocky crest of Tom Heights, with its magnificent views, at a small cairn.

3   Continue along the undulating crest of the fell to a larger cairn, and on again to a third cairn, and here turn right (north east) and descend to a stile over a wall to a track beyond.

4   Go left on a descending track between walls, now heading for Oxen Fell and High Cross at the main road.

5   Cross the main road and take a signposted path, right, through larch trees, then along a field edge, beside a wall, to a ladder stile. Over the stile, turn left along a narrow road that leads to High Park.

6   At High Park continue along the road for 150m/yds to a signposted footpath on the left. Climb with the path beside trees, turning right above bracken to reach a wall end. Here a step stile crosses a fence and a mound of volcanic material can be used to cross a stretch of boggy ground to rejoin the path.

7   When a well-defined path branches left, follow it, keeping to the dry ground, and head for a gate and a track into woodland, on the way passing a long-forgotten bracken cutter. In the woodland, follow the track to a group of houses, Hodge Close. Pass the first house on your right, then bear left on rising ground to a garage.

8   Directly opposite the garage, descend on an old quarry tram-way, now a well-worn stone path, to reach the quarry floor. The path leads you to the huge arched entrance into Hodge Close, but do not be tempted to explore much further. Retrace your steps to the garage.

9   From the garage, take the gated track on the right to pass a reed-filled dam, continuing to a gate on your right. Go through the gate and follow a track with a fence on the right. Descend to another gate, but don't go through this one.

10 Turn left on an ascending track to yet another gate. You can

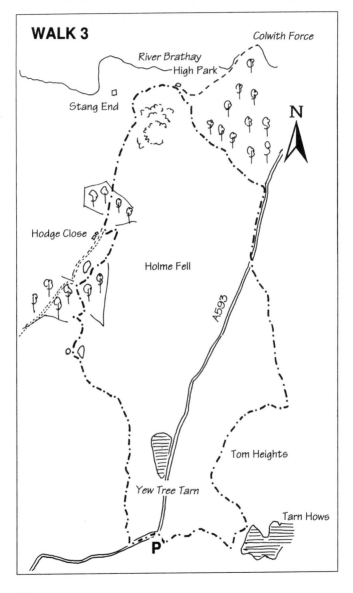

WALK 3

Colwith Force

River Brathay

High Park

Stang End

N

Hodge Close

Holme Fell

A593

Yew Tree Tarn

Tom Heights

Tarn Hows

P

go through this one, after which, at the top of the climb, take the track running back, left, into a quarry.

- ### Hodge Close Quarry
- *Many of the small quarries to be seen in the Lakeland fells were*
- *to supply stone for local wall building. Most builders recycled*
- *stone, which was a fifth of the price of new stone, but as building*
- *increased so the demand for stone and roofing slate grew.*
- *Hodge Close supplied both to the local trade and much further*
- *afield.*
-
- *Today the quarry is a playground for rock climbers, and the*
- *deep waters entertain sub aqua divers who explore the many*
- *side tunnels. What is especially pleasing, however, is to see the*
- *way nature has started to recolonise the workings with oak,*
- *birch and hazel.*

11 From the quarry, take the second path on your right, ascending to a small disused reservoir, and here bear right, crossing the dam, and follow the water's edge to a boggy gully opposite the dam.

12 Keep as much as possible to dry ground, and turn right (south-southeast) alongside the gully, and aim for a col on the skyline. When you reach it, cross a collapsed wall, and begin descending a stony path, passing a large boulder to a large cairn.

13 From the cairn, white arrows waymark the route, via a gate and stile, to Yew Tree Farm, with its fine spinning gallery, used for the drying of wool and yarn.

14 Go past the farm to the road, and there cross the road to a gate. Through the gate, turn left, and go along a field edge to a gate giving into the car park.

- ### Bracken harvest
- *Until recent times, bracken was harvested for use as animal*
- *bedding, thatching and making potash. Much of the machinery*
- *used for the harvest is still to be found on the fells, only to be*
- *reclaimed when a tenant farmer sells up and needs to recover*
- *his money.*

4

Old Man of Coniston

*Until twenty or so years ago, the Old Man of Coniston
was the highest summit in Lancashire, then it was
transferred, with a great swathe of Lancashire-over-the-
Sands, to Cumbria.*

*The distinction brought many walkers to its summit, but
the dictates of bureaucracy have scarcely lessened the
attention this distinguished summit receives.*

*Today, this the most southerly of the high Lakeland fells,
still attracts walkers every day of the year.*

*The following walk briefly visits old quarry workings which
extracted a most beautiful green slate from the
mountain for more than three centuries, before calling at
a high mountain tarn set in a steep-sided cradle directly
beneath the summit.*

Start: Disused quarry, Walna Scar Road. GR289970
Total distance: 7½km (4¾ miles)
Height gain: 590m (1,935 feet)
Difficulty: A rewarding walk that will be a good test of
most children's temperament and determination. Not to
be tackled in poor visibility. The summit is very close to
the edge of a steep drop.

Young children will find the final, steep section strenu-
ous. If in doubt, the best approach is to plan only to go
as far as Low Water, to have a good rest while watching
others toil up the slopes, and then decide whether to try
them yourself.

*The start of the walk is reached by a climbing drive from Coniston,
by a narrow road behind the railway station. When this road passes
through an intake gate to open fell you will find the quarry parking
space a short distance ahead, on the left.*

1   Leave the parking area and head back towards the gate, there

turning left to walk easily along a broad track (signposted: Coniston Old Man, Low Water). The track starts alongside a wall, which quickly falls away to the right, while the track climbs gradually for almost a mile to a sharp left turn at the back of a rocky mound. Ignore any paths on the right, but follow the main trail as it climbs roughly, twisting about as it meets the first of many slate spoil heaps.

2   The spoil heaps are not an attractive sight, but they remain an important part of our industrial heritage. It would be nice if someone put all the slate back where it came from; meanwhile we must accept it for what it is, industrial archaeology.

3   The upward path is never in doubt. Across the base of spoil heaps, it becomes loose underfoot, and slippery in wet conditions. As you climb beside a slate wall you pass beneath steel hawsers that where used to convey slate to the valley. Soon, at a bend, you encounter the remains of quarry sheds that are worth a moment's investigation, but do resist the temptation to explore any mining levels you find burrowing into the hillside, they are now all dangerous.

4   Continue ever upwards, passing more cables, until, just before your third encounter with these rusting remnants you can take a path, right, climbing to a narrow col, beyond which lies Low Water.

A word of warning is needed! Do not go beneath the third set of cables. A large cave-like quarry lies beyond, but this has seen many roof-falls in recent years and is now most unstable and unsafe. Make sure young children do not run on ahead.

- *Slate quarries*

  Slate has been quarried from the Old Man for over three centuries, yielding large quantities of high quality green slate which was in demand all around the world as a building material. The walk passes the remains of dressing sheds and winch wheel housings, and there are many tunnels used by the miners. Many of these have wooden floors covered with rubble, and most are now rotten; a fall of some hundreds of feet awaits the incautious.

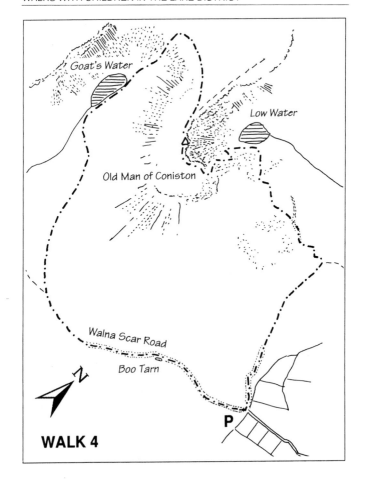

WALK 4

5   When you reach Low Water you can cross the outflow and find a comfortable spot on the opposite bank from which to assess your enthusiasm for the steep pull to the summit which lies beyond.

6   Returning to the main path, follow it upwards in zigzags. The last section is a little loose and eroded, but will not cause problems for carefully-placed feet. On reaching more level ground, a broad

path climbs less steeply to the summit plateau, crowned by a large cairn on a plinth, and a trig pillar very close to the edge of the corrie housing Low Water. Keep children under close supervision at this point.

7   A simple retracing of steps, taking care on the descent to Low Water, is the quickest way back.

8   For a longer circuit, and a splendid way of concluding the walk, leave the summit, keeping the corrie rim on your right, but keep a look out for a cairn at the start of a descending path on the left. This leads down a rocky pathway to reach a high mountain pass, Goat's Hawse, rather a wet place to be.

9   Before getting too embroiled in the bogginess, go left, down a good, but loose, path to reach the end of Goat's Water, a magnificent mountain lake set most dramatically beneath the towering cliffs of Dow Crag.

10 Follow the path through the boulders at the water's edge, gradually leaving the lake behind to cross a low rocky rib that has a moment or two of downward squirming (all avoidable) before following an easy course to a large cairn at its junction with the Walna Scar Road. Turn left, and follow the road (a motorable highway, though not a recommended one) back to the starting point, passing diminutive, reed-filled Boo Tarn on the way.

The Old Man of Coniston
The first accepted tourist ascent of the Old Man is accorded to Captain Joseph Budworth, in 1792. On what was jokingly called a 'rest day' from his travels, he had already walked from Ambleside to look at Coniston Water. Unable to resist the challenge of the mountain, and sustained only by brandy, he made the first ascent...and still made it back to Ambleside.

5

Wetherlam from Tilberthwaite

This fine, but energetic, ascent of Wetherlam from Tilberthwaite is a popular walk and well within the capabilities of most children, though some previous upland experience would be an advantage.

Tilberthwaite Gill is a chasm of great natural beauty, a deep gash in the landscape hidden among the hills and unseen from the roadway. It is a spot that was tremendously popular with Victorian visitors who linked precarious footpaths and rickety wooden bridges to view the spectacle.

The featureless top of Wetherlam makes this an inappropriate walk in poor visibility.

Start: Car park, Tilberthwaite. GR306010
Total distance: 7½km (4½ miles)
Height gain: 572m (1,875 feet)
Difficulty: Most of the walk is on well-made miners' tracks, finishing by a rocky pull to the summit. The return is by a grassy plateau and a green path beside Crook Beck. The height gain may prove too much for very young children, and a few adults! — though this is a fine outing on which to introduce children to sustained uphill work. Well-timed words of encouragement will work wonders.

1   Leave the car park by the steps to gain a signposted footpath ascending quarry spoil to a path junction beside a hut ruin. Near the ruin, the second entrance on your left gives a view into Penny Rigg Quarry, its vertical edge much favoured by rock climbers, but no place for young children.

2   Take the right hand path which sets off level, then descends by steps to a bridge over the bubbling waters of Tilberthwaite Gill.

3   Cross the bridge to a sign warning that the footpath is steep and dangerous beyond this point, so great care is needed here for a short while. Use the path to climb out of the gill, over a stile and continue climbing to join a miner's track.

- ***Tilberthwaite Gill***
- *In spite of the numerous relics of former mining activity, the*
- *whole area around Tilberthwaite is outstandingly beautiful, and*
- *was a place of popular resort for the Victorians, who contrived*
- *a series of wooden bridges to gain a better view of the falls in*
- *Tilberthwaite Gill. Most of these additions disappeared during*
- *the last war as a result of army training.*
- *Penny Rigg Quarry was worked for copper ore and, later,*
- *green slate. Around 1875 the quarry was flooded to provide*
- *water power to Penny Rigg Mill.*

4   Here turn left, with the track running close by the ravine in which cascading water can be heard but is obscured from view by trees. At a junction bear right, keeping to the main path to reach a small side stream.

5   As you step over the stream note to your left the ruins of the old Tilberthwaite Mine and its yellow-brown copper spoil tips. This mine is especially dangerous, some of the shafts being over 500 feet deep.

6   Continue along the track as it climbs gently to more waste tips and ruined cabins at Hellen's Mine. From here the track skirts the wet basin of the wettest Dry Cove in Lakeland to reach Borlase Mine.

- ***Dry Cove***
- *Dry Cove was dammed and flooded to provide a head of water*
- *to power a water wheel at the Tilberthwaite Mine, which can be*
- *seen nearby. There are many dangerous, deep shafts here,*
- *along with the remains of offices, a wheelhouse and a crushing*
- *mill.*
- *The track beside the cove leads to Hellen's Mine, the*
- *entrance to which now issues water. On the opposite side of*

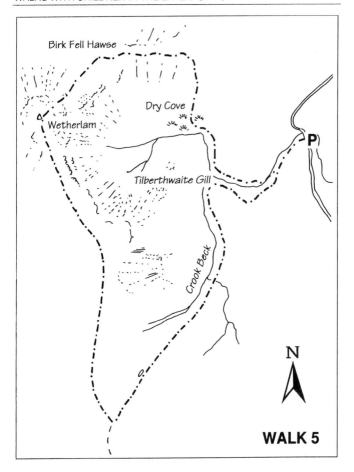

WALK 5

- the cove you can seen Man Arm Mine, so named because of
- a kink in the main vein.
- Near Borlase Mine stands a paraffin-engined air compressor
- used for power tools until the mine closed in the 1930s.

7 From the mine take a rough path ascending, right, in zigzags between rock outcrops to Birk Fell Hawes, a narrow col between Birk Fell and Wetherlam.

8   Once you reach the Hawse, and after a moment's rest (well-earned) set of southwest for a delightful and easy scramble up Wetherlam Edge to the summit of Wetherlam.

- *The summit is adorned with much rock, pale grey in colour, in*
- *which you can detect the same colouration as in the spoil heaps*
- *below, and among which you can find numerous comfortable*
- *places to relax and recover from the ascent.*
- *The highest point is marked by a large cairn, and from it you*
- *can pick out distant Ingleborough, in the district of Craven, one*
- *of Yorkshire's 'Three Peaks'.*

9   Leave the fell top in a roughly southeasterly direction, crossing the grassy plateau to a large cairn, that marks the start of a distinct cairned path descending for some distance to a small tarn at the top of Hole Rake Pass.

10 At the tarn turn left (northeast) on a grassy track, continue past a quarry entrance, and descend alongside Crook Beck, which is contained in a pleasant gill.

11 Step over a small beck above a rowan-lined waterfall, and keep with the cairned path to a large cairn at a stream crossing. Here, turn right on a path to circle above the slopes of Tilberthwaite Gill.

12 Pass a small cairn on a waste heap, to reach a rocky step across a small side stream. Press on to the hut ruin encountered at the start of the walk, and from there retrace your steps to the car park.

Slate quarrying
Though lacking the 'glamour' of mineral mines, slate quarrying has played an immensely important part in the economy of the Lake District.

Even so, it is a robber industry, in the sense that you cannot replace what is taken away, and great spoil heaps are left to mar the landscape for all eternity.

6

Greenburn Copper Mine and The Cathedral

The wild and isolated valley of Greenburn, once home to one of Lakeland's major copper mines and a place of much industry and business, is now quiet and seldom-visited.

The stream bank between the mine workings and the dammed tarn has many pleasant picnic sites and small rock pools, though care needs to be exercised in the vicinity of the mines, where there are many open shafts. There is much of fascination here, but all children must be closely supervised and kept well away from mine shafts and inviting pools of water.

Start: Tilberthwaite car park. GR306010
Total distance: 8km (5 miles)
Height gain: 590m (1,935 feet)
Difficulty: A pleasant walk using old mine tracks and steep fellside paths. The visit to Cathedral quarry entails the use of stepping stones along a short wet tunnel. There is always an element of risk in the vicinity of any Lakeland quarry or mine, and Greenburn is no exception.
Young children must be closely supervised.

1   Leave Tilberthwaite car park by the steps, and follow the directions given in Walk 5 as far as Hellen's Mine.

2   At Hellen's Mine, turn right (northeast), passing old cabins and a partially blocked shaft, to a col boasting a stand of windswept Scots pines that are reason enough for a moment's pause.

3   Descend from the col among tree stumps to a tree-lined hollow containing a small bog. Turn left, keeping the bog and a fence on

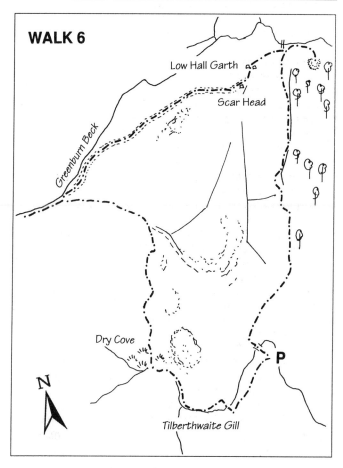

WALK 6

Low Hall Garth

Scar Head

Greenburn Beck

Dry Cove

N

Tilberthwaite Gill

P

your left, and continue, ignoring two stiles, descending alongside the fence as it turns right (east) towards a wall junction.

4   Cross the fence by a stile about 100m/yds before the wall, and head (northwards) towards a grassy mound close by the wall. Now follow the wall (northeast) descending past a stile to a track in the valley bottom. An expanse of ground just before the track is very wet, but can be avoided on the left, joining the track 100m/yds from

a gate. Once on the track, turn left (west) and follow it to the remains of Greenburn Mine.

- ### Greenburn Mine
  The mine extracted copper from seven veins, with the greatest period of prosperity coming between 1854 and 1861, when more than a thousand tons of ore were extracted. The seven mile journey to the rail head at Coniston ultimately made the mine uneconomic.

  Among the ruined buildings it is still possible to identify the dressing floors and two water wheels. The reservoir dam was breached by the same heavy storm which in August 1966 destroyed Stockley Bridge in upper Borrowdale. Here it caused severe damage to the mine site and to farms downstream.

5 If you bear left at a junction before the mine, you can walk among the ruined mine buildings. If you go right, you cross a stream flowing from the mine ruins to follow a path beside Greenburn Beck to the dam of Greenburn Reservoir. The grassy stream banks are an ideal place for lunch.

6 Return to the main track and head (east) out of the valley. At the gate, cross the stile and continue on the track to a junction.

7 Bear right and go past the next turning on the right, continuing to a gate and walled track. Through the gate, follow the track past two cottages, High and Low Hall Garth, to a wooden gate. Go through the gate for about 100m/yds to a rising track and gate on the right. Take this track to a flat area where, on your right, you find the dark entrance to a tunnel. Go through the tunnel using stepping stones to reach the large amphitheatre of Cathedral Quarry.

**DO NOT GO PAST THE CENTRAL PILLAR, THERE IS A
VERY DEEP WATER-FILLED SHAFT BEYOND.
DO NOT CLIMB ON THE BOULDERS, THEY ARE UNSAFE**

- ### The Cathedral
  This large cavern was worked by quarrymen known locally as 'Old Men', who would have worked by candlelight on wooden platforms, never able to see as a whole the vast cathedral-like

- *cavern with its central pillar they had created. The hole now*
- *allowing in light was made by later workings above, while the*
- *water beyond fills a deep shaft to lower levels.*

8 Return to the tunnel entrance and take the descending track on the left to return to the gate on the main track.

9 Go through the gate and after about 75m/yds, take a quarry track on your left. At a flat area turn left to a gate and footpath sign. Follow the path, climbing a steep meadow to cross the top wall by a step and gap stile.

10 Keeping a wall on your left continue (south) up the fell to ruined huts, and here bear right (southwest) to pick up a track near a gate. Turn left (south) to pass through the gate and press on along the track to High Tilberthwaite Farm, followed by a short stretch of road walking to reach the car park.

Stope and feather mining

Levels were cut through the rock by miners with 'stope and feather', implements consisting of two thin pieces of iron, called feathers, about six inches long and half an inch broad, flat on one side and round on the other, and a thin tapering wedge, or stope, of the same length and width. A hole was bored in the rock and the feathers placed in it; the point of the stope was then introduced between them and driven in with a hammer until the rock was rent. This would have been a slow and laborious process, and the old miners needed to be expert in the use of these tools.

7

Tarn Hows via Tom Gill

The Tarns, or Tarn Hows, must be one of the most beautiful and much-visited places in southern Lakeland. The most common approach, by car from Hawkshead, poses problems along the narrow lanes. By contrast this walk from the main Coniston to Ambleside road has no such difficulties, and ascends through the wooded ravine of Tom Gill with its waterfalls and rocky cascades. The first glimpse of the tarn as your head rises above the small dam will linger in your memory for years to come, and encourage many revisits.

Start: Glen Mary Bridge. GR322999
Total distance: 4km (2½ miles)
Height gain: 150m (490 feet)
Difficulty: An easy walk, ideal for children who have not done much walking. The ascent, on a rough and stony path, crosses a few unbridged streams, but the walk around the tarn is on a well-maintained path, constructed with handicapped visitors in mind.

1   Leave the parking area by crossing the wooden bridge span-ning Tom Gill. Turn right on a terraced path to follow the Gill upstream. When you come level with the waterfalls take the lower path for a closer look at the falls. From here a well-made path continues by crossing a rocky outcrop to a small moss-covered dam and the tarn outflow.

- **Tom Gill**
- This little oak-lined ravine with a small waterfall, cascades and
- rock pools carries the outflow from the tarns, and was renamed
- by John Ruskin, who lived nearby at Brantwood. Not satisfied
- with the name, Tom Gill, for such a beautiful spot, Ruskin
- renamed it 'Glen Mary', which touched a note of accord with the
- public, and explains the name of the 'Glen Mary bridge' on the
- main road.

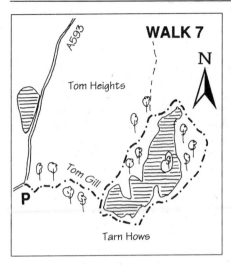

WALK 7

N

Tom Heights

Tom Gill

P

Tarn Hows

2   At no point during this ascent should you cross the stream; there are no stiles over the wall or fence higher up to enable you to get back.

3   Above the dam turn left on a well-maintained path that forms part of the Cumbria Way. Keep with the main track (waymarked) at any turnings on the left. Go through a gate and follow a barbed wire fence to a wooden bridge, after which the track ascends to a junction. Continue ahead (waymarked).

4   The way now crosses open ground with views over the tarn, and numerous pleasant picnic spots away from the crowds that gather around the car parks.

5   At another gate continue with the track until, after passing a stand of pine trees on your right, you can turn right on a path crossing grassy slopes above the tarn to bring you on to a track leading back to the outflow.

6   Turning left, away from the tarn, ascend the track for 50m/yds to a grassy track on your right. The way descends alongside a wall, passing through groups of larch and oak trees to a field gate. Go through the gate, keep the wall on your right, and descend on a grassy trod to the overgrown remains of Lane Head Farm. Turn sharp right and cross a field to another gate, beyond which a stony lane will lead you back to the start.

8
White Maiden from Torver

*White Maiden and nearby White Pike are seldom
visited by walkers, so this walk provides an opportunity
to wander across trackless fells, and to practice
navigation techniques.
The view from White Maiden is extensive and embraces
the dark form of Black Combe, the silver sands of the
Duddon estuary, Scafell Pike, and, on a clear day,
Ingleborough in the Yorkshire Dales.*

Start: Layby on the A593, near track junction.
GR285945
Total distance: 10½km (6½ miles)
Height gain: 540m (1,770 feet)
Difficulty: Moderate; the walk uses stone tracks and
good paths to the top of Walna Scar Pass, and then
crosses open country without clear pathways. As a
result the walk is not recommended on days of poor
visibility.

1 Leave the layby parking area by a tarmac track signposted for
Coniston Old Man and Walna Scar. The track is waymarked
through the village of Scar Head and leads to a walled bridleway.

2 Follow the bridleway through two gates and past a stone barn
to a third gate. Go through this gate also and on over a bridge
spanning Tranearth Beck, then keep ahead on a rough track to
gated sheep pens, following blue arrow markers through the pens.
Turn sharp right to a wooden bridge over Torver Beck.

3 Once over the beck, turn left to pass between quarry waste
heaps and climb beside a tree-lined gully. Care is needed just here
because the gully is the entrance to a quarry and has steep and
loose sides.

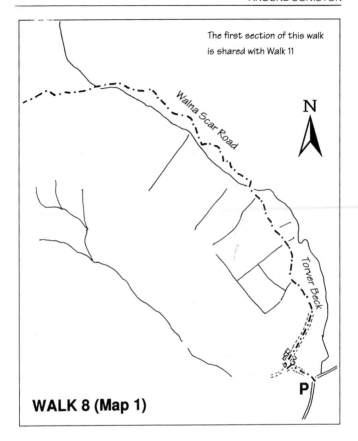

The first section of this walk
is shared with Walk 11

Walna Scar Road

Torver Beck

N

WALK 8 (Map 1)

P

4 Climb to a wire fence, turn right to circle around the edge of Bannishead Quarry. Of the grass paths that then appear ahead, take that on the left and climb easily to Walna Scar Road. (Ignore the prominent large cairn, which marks the start of a path to Goat's Water).

5 Turn left along the Walna Scar Road to cross a packhorse bridge over Torver Beck beyond which the trail is rather more eroded as it climbs to a large cairn.

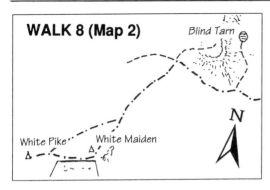

WALK 8 (Map 2)

Blind Tarn

White Pike   *White Maiden*

N

Optional extra:
At the large cairn you can leave the main track for a wet, but improving, path that ascends to an old quarry. As you reach the quarry spoil, leave it, right, aiming for a notch on the skyline ahead through which you will discover Blind Tarn, concealed in a glacial corrie below the dark crags of Brown Pike and Buck Pike. The tarn is 'blind' because it has no outflow, and its banks make a delightful and sheltered spot for lunch. You must then return to the main track.

To continue:
6   Follow the Walna Scar track past a number of smaller cairns and a small stone shelter on the right — a couple of very close friends might just squeeze in there in an emergency!

7   A small cairn to the right of the path marks the top of the pass, so here, turn left to climb the grassy fellside (no path) to a cairn marking the summit of a grassy ridge, Walna Scar. Continuing southwest a path does now lead you to a shallow col from which you can climb another grassy slope to the unexpectedly rocky summit of White Maiden, its cairn close by the angle of a wall, and overlooking the sweeping expanse of Torver High Common.

8   To return, simply retrace your steps, no less an enjoyable experience for treading familiar ground. In the lee of Walna Scar, on perfect days, you can wile away much time comfortably resting against a boulder, listening to the sound of silence.

9

Monk Coniston Moor

*The oak forest of Monk Coniston Moor was coppiced
during the sixteenth and seventeenth centuries to
produce charcoal which was then used in bloomeries
where ore was smelted, or for making gunpowder.
These delightful woodlands have now been absorbed by
the Forestry Commission into the Forest of Grisedale,
and this walk takes you along quiet tracks, away from
the main visitor areas, and affords splendid views across
Coniston Water.*

Start: Water Head car park. GR316978
Total distance: 9½km (6 miles)
Height gain: 270m (885 feet)
Difficulty: Easy walking along forest trails, wet in
places. Care is needed on the final busy road section.

1   At the car park entrance turn right along the road a short
distance to a right-hand bend. Cross the road to a signposted
footpath, and follow a fence-lined path (east).

2   At the end of the path, cross a stile and turn left to follow a well-
signposted footpath diversion, first around the edge of a field, then
through the garden of Rowlinson Ground. The diversion ends
down steps to the house access drive, there turning left.

3   Follow the signs for Hawkshead, and through the drive gates
turn left on to the road, shortly passing an old slate fence to reach
a track on the right.

4   Turn right (south) along the track and go through a gate onto
a forest trail. Walk along the trail, taking the left branch at the first
junction. Keep to the main trail when a grass track leaves on the
left, and continue with a fence on your right to the next turning left,

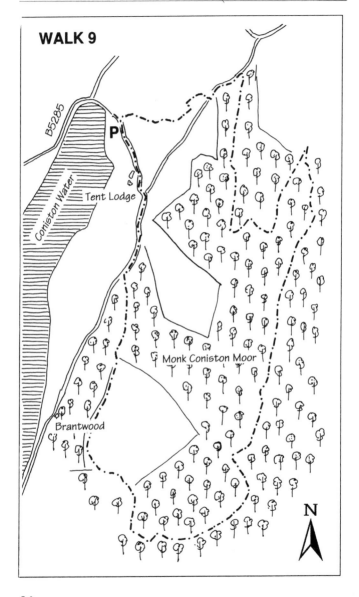

WALK 9

B5285

P

Coniston Water

Tent Lodge

Monk Coniston Moor

Brantwood

N

opposite a ladder stile grass track on the right.

5   Follow the trail to the left as it climbs in zigzags past wind-damaged trees (tarn below to the left) to a T-junction. Turn left and follow the trail to a clearing on the left. After 75m/yds, take a turning back to the right on an ascending track, and follow the trail to another T-junction, passing en route through two deer gates.

6   At the junction turn right along a track, and take a gated path, directly ahead as the trail bends to the left.

7   Now on a clear path follow an electricity line to a gate onto a track, there turning left and then right and go past an aerial mast. As the track bends to the right leave it, left, on a footpath.

8   This new path, wet for a while, soon climbs to dry ground and passes a larger aerial mast. Go across the access track and continue on a path that now follows slate posts that mark the line of an old boundary fence. Pass to the left and right of two small tarns to meet a track.

9   Turn left, passing two tracks to the left, rising gently to the brow of a hill, and then descending right, through trees on a rough path to the buildings at Lawson Park.

10 Cross the access track to a path (signpost ed to Coniston), and follow a descending track through a gate, accompanying a stone wall to a bridge and past a barn.

11 Pleasant birch woodland ensues, through which the trail continues to a gate at the road.

12 Turn right along the road, taking care not to tangle with traffic on this busy back road, until you return to the car park.

10

Coniston Bloomery

Encouraged by the monks of Furness Abbey, the woodlands of south Lakeland were burned for charcoal to be used in bloomeries for the smelting of iron ore, most notably from medieval times until the seventeenth-century.
This pleasant walk visits Coniston Hall, the oldest building in Coniston, and then meanders along the wooded shore of Coniston Water to the site of a bloomery that
flourished here 400 years or so ago. The walk returns to Coniston along the trackbed of the disused Furness Railway.

Start: Coniston main car park. GR303976
Total distance: 9km (5½ miles)
Height gain: 110m (360 feet)
Difficulty: An easy walk along well-signposted paths and tracks, with only a few unbridged streams to negotiate.

1   Leave the car park, turning left in front of the church to the bridge spanning Church Beck. Cross the bridge, go left, past the petrol station, to the next turning on the left (signposted: Gondola).

2   Turn left here and follow the road for 400m/yds until the road turns sharply left. At this point cross the road to a step stile and a signposted footpath. Turn right along a grassy path beside a hedge, to a gate. Now, with a fence on your left, the path takes you to a broad track heading for Coniston Hall.

3   In the grounds of Coniston Hall, follow signposts, right then left, to a camp site, and when in the camping field, take the first available track on your left. This will take you down to the lakeshore, heading southwest to a small gate in a wall.

- ### *Coniston Hall*
- *This charming building was built in the fifteenth-century by the*
- *Flemings, and there is evidence of an earlier hall on the site.*
- *Certainly, W.G. Collingwood comments that Coniston Hall was*
- *"the seat of the Flemings from about 1250 to some time after*
- *1700", the family having gained Coniston in 1250 by marriage,*
- *making it their principal seat for seven generations. Sir Daniel*
- *Fleming was born of the Coniston family in 1633. He went to*
- *Queen's College, Oxford, and to Gray's Inn, and followed his*
- *father in the cause of King Charles, losing much in pocket and*
- *his prospects. So he left Coniston Hall and moved to Rydal,*
- *which had been the Fleming's second home since about 1484.*

4   From the wall, the lush green field you see in front of you is the site of the Coniston bloomery, and was once covered with ash and waste heaps from the smelting process.

5   Stay along the lakeshore, heading for a step stile leading into another camp site, and stay with the shore (waymarked) passing a slipway to a track leading into Torver Common Wood. Use the broad track into the woodland, staying close by the lake, and crossing a small stream until a sign directs you left on a path to a clearing and a signpost for Torver.

6   To return, turn right (west), and on a broad clear path cross a vehicle track and go through a collapsed wall, after which the path is enclosed by trees and climbs to a gate and signpost (Torver Commons).

7   Go through the gate on to a track leading to a gate beside a barn. Beyond the gate, follow an enclosed track leading to another gate and a stile. Over the stile, turn right, through a gate, and then by a hawthorn-lined green path cross four gated fields. At the fifth field head for a wall corner directly opposite, and follow the wall, right, for a few strides to a gap stile. Beyond the stile take a clear path for 100m/yds through a conifer plantation to a field. Cross a fence and turn right along the edge of the woodland at the rear of Hoathwaite Farm.

8   The on-going path takes you through gated sheep pens to the

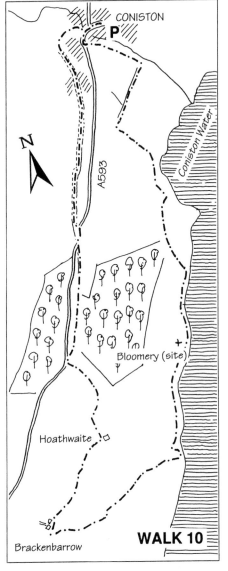

farmyard. Turn left out of the farm and at the entrance take the gate on your right into a camping field.

9 Cross the top of the field with the fence on your left, and go past a cattle grid until you reach a grass track descending to a beck and gate into a larch woodland. Stay with the track beside the beck to a ladder stile, and go over the stile to cross the beck by a bridge.

10 The way now follows a grass track, at times indistinctly, but setting off ahead, then bearing left to follow the base of rising ground (do not head for the caravans that can be seen among the trees to the right) to a gate in a wall. The gate gives access to the old Furness railway track, and once through it turn right to follow waymarking past the caravan site entrance, then

by a grassy track to a gate beside a seat. The gate leads to a narrow road. Follow this for 100m/yds until the road bends sharply to the right. The onward route is the signposted track on the left, leading back on to the course of the old railway.

11 The trackbed is now followed back to Coniston, its tree-lined course giving splendid views of Coniston Water and the tree-cloaked hills beyond. Shortly after passing under an arched slate bridge you arrive at a new housing estate on the site of Coniston station. Follow the on-going path to join a road past small workshops and the mountain rescue post to a junction.

12 Turn right on a descending road past the Sun Hotel to the Church Beck bridge. Cross the beck by a footbridge and go past the church to return to the car park.

- ***Coniston forest***
- *When the Norse people first settled among the fells of Furness,*
- *and around the great lake which they named Thorstanes*
- *Watter, the valley and lower fells of Coniston were dense with*
- *growths of oak, holly, ash, hazel and birch. By the sixteenth*
- *century all this had gone, and of the great oak woods there*
- *remained but a few scattered trees and the enormous beams*
- *in such buildings as Coniston Old Hall. By the time of Henry VIII*
- *all the fells were bare of timber, the forests all but gone, leaving*
- *"lytell short Okes...[but] no Tymber of any valewe."*
-
- ***Bloomeries***
- *So important was the charcoal available from the Furness*
- *woods that many bloomery sites are found near to the timber*
- *source rather than the iron mine. The iron probably came up*
- *the lake or on packhorses to the smithies which were also*
- *located near fast-flowing streams which provided the water*
- *power.*

11
Dow Crag and Goat's Water

This is a pleasant but challenging walk making use of old quarry tracks to gain height to the top of Walna Scar, a high mountain pass linking Coniston with Dunnerdale. The way continues along a fine rocky ridge to the top of Dow Crag overlooking Goat's Water, by way of which the walk concludes.

This is an outstanding excursion for youngsters, a full mountaineering walk, and sure to give them immense satisfaction, but it may be beyond very young children.

Start: Layby on the A593, near track junction.
GR285945
Total distance: 11km (7 miles)
Height gain: 670m (2,195 feet)
Difficulty: Demanding, and with considerable height gain, but an excellent introduction to high fell walking. A fine clear day is required.

1   Leave the layby along the tarmac track signposted to Coniston Old Man and Walna Scar. Follow the waymarking through the village of Scar Head to join a walled bridleway. Walk on, to the third gate spanning the track, and there go through a gate to cross a bridge spanning Tranearth Beck, then by a rough track to gated sheep pens. Blue waymarking now directs you to a wooden bridge over Torver Beck. Once across the bridge turn left to pass between quarry waste heaps, then climb beside a tree-lined gully, the entrance to quarry workings, and dangerous.

2   Climb to a wire fence, turn right to circle the edge of the quarry, and on the opposite side take a terraced path to the left, climbing to the Walna Scar road. Turn left to cross a packhorse bridge over Torver Beck. Once across the bridge the track becomes more eroded as it climbs to a large cairn.

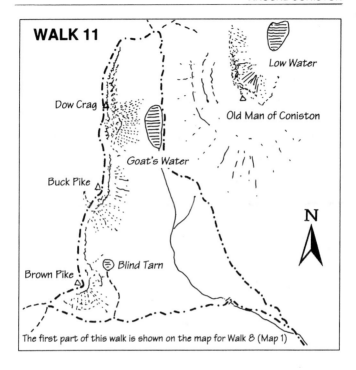

WALK 11

Low Water

Dow Crag

Old Man of Coniston

Goat's Water

Buck Pike

N

Brown Pike

Blind Tarn

The first part of this walk is shown on the map for Walk 8 (Map 1)

3   Continue, ascending all the while, passing small cairns and a small stone shelter on the right.

- ***Walna Scar Road***
- *This is an ancient packhorse route crossing the southern end*
- *of the Coniston range at 2000 feet, and linking the copper*
- *mines of Coniston with Seathwaite in the Duddon valley. The*
- *route also served many of the high fell quarries on Torver*
- *Common during the prosperous years of the mines. It was*
- *improved for use by carts, but today is suitable only for walkers,*
- *though it occasionally attracts kamikaze motor cyclists.*

4   A small cairn marks the top of the Walna Scar road, a high mountain pass from which there is a fine view down into Dunnerdale. Turn right and ascend on a grassy path to a stone shelter on the

top of Brown Pike, the first of two fell tops en route to Dow Crag. From here on the views are consistently impressive, and the high level walking of supreme quality.

5   From the shelter the path heads north along the rim of the corrie that houses Blind Tarn (Walk 8 describes a route to the tarn from the Walna Scar road).

6   Press on along the ridge, crossing another minor summit, Buck Pike, on the way, and then heading for Dow Crag by a stony path. As you approach Dow Crag, the immense cliffs falling to Goat's Water below become more pronounced and the path crosses the top of one or two yawning gullies; children will need close supervision here, and whilst on the fine rocky summit of Dow Crag.

7   From this point everything is downhill, but only physically. You may be leaving behind the magnificent views from the top of Dow Crag, but the return beside Goat's Water is walking of the highest order.

8   From the top of Dow Crag go north, continuing your original direction, on a clear rocky path which soon turns northeast to descend to Goat's Hawse, a boggy col linking Dow Crag and the Old Man of Coniston.

9   Go down to the Hawse and as the path starts to ascend on the other side take a path off to the right and descend to Goat's Water. The path is loose and slippery in places.

10 Use the path along the left shore of Goat's Water, passing through scattered boulders, and following a good path that leads all the way out of the valley, to a cairn on the Walna Scar road, not far from the point at which you first joined it.

11 Cross the track to a green path, and descend to the wire fencing around Bannishead Quarry, from where you retrace your steps to Torver.

12

Boulder valley and Levers Water

Starting from the Walna Scar Road, this pleasant walk on little-used paths threads a way through a valley of large boulders deposited by a retreating glacier at the end of the last Ice Age, about 10,000 years ago. With many places at which to stop for lunch, the walk continues to Levers Water, and returns through Coppermines valley, scene of much fascinating industrial activity in ages gone by.

Start: Disused quarry, Walna Scar road. GR289970
Total distance: 6km (4 miles)
Height gain: 290m (950 feet)
Difficulty: A pleasant walk using old quarry tracks and clear footpaths, but flanked by many deep mine shafts.

1   Leave the parking area on a broad track heading northwest alongside a wall, which falls away as the track climbs. After about a mile the track turns sharply to the left around a rocky mound. As it does, take the second path on the right, a terraced track high above Coppermines valley, which takes you on, past the entrance to an old mine.

2   As you pass the mine entrance the track ends, and you should follow a path past a large boulder, known as the Pudding Stone, to descend to a wooden bridge crossing Low Water Beck. Beyond lies Boulder Valley.

3   Cross the bridge, and follow a rocky path ascending on the right of the valley. As you climb, make for a large boulder perched on a col on the skyline. From the col, descend, passing en route a number of mine shafts enclosed by wire fences, to meet the shore path of Levers Water. Now turn right past the fenced entrance to Simon's Mine (do not cross the fence, the ground on the other side

43

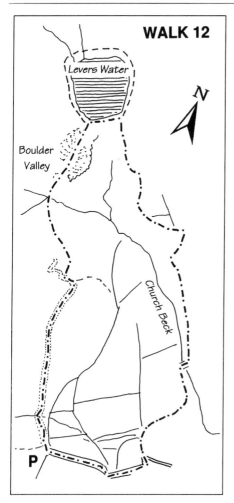

WALK 12

Levers Water

Boulder Valley

Church Beck

P

is loose and unstable, and the mine more than 450 feet deep!). Cross Lever's Water dam and a causeway to a track descending on the right.

Optional extra:
When you meet the shore path at Lever's Water you can turn left to follow a clear path all the way round the tarn until you reach the causeway.

4   To return, follow the broad descending track (southeast) to a row of iron posts crossing the track. The track here swings right, but you continue ahead to a broad green path. The path descends, then turns left, with a descending path to the right. Take this path on the right, surmounting a small rock step and then continuing through bracken to the rear of a slate building.

- *You are now in Coppermines Valley which during the 1800s*
- *was a scene of much activity, with crushing and sorting sheds,*
- *and mine offices. Today most of these buildings have gone, but*

- *a private venture is undertaking restoration work to produce a*
- *heritage site.*
-
- ### Coppermines valley
- *To encourage mining production, royal patronage was granted*
- *by Elizabeth I by the setting up in 1561 of the Society for the*
- *Mines Royal. The mines of the Coniston fells saw large-scale*
- *exploitation from 1599 onwards, the main mine lying in Church*
- *Beck, though this first start ended in 1650. In 1758 the*
- *Macclesfield Copper Company obtained the lease of the*
- *Coniston mines, worked them for a while until all the known ore*
- *bodies were worked out. In 1830, a Cornish tin miner, John*
- *Barratt, arrived with new knowledge and techniques, and*
- *quickly stepped up production. By 1849 the Coniston Mining*
- *Company employed 400 men and was removing about 250*
- *tons of ore a month.*
- *All was not sweetness and light, however, for in 1620 there*
- *was a complaint at Coniston concerning "both meadowe and*
- *Cornelande as is decayed and wasted"owing to the pollution of*
- *the Church Beck "by Reasone of the Stamphowse and brayings*
- *of the Coper vre [ore] and other Rubbishe at the saide*
- *Stamphowse".*

5   Turn right on a track through the heritage site to a gate between two white buildings. Go through the gate and follow the track to the left, then turn right to pass a row of cottages (Irish Row) on your left. Keep with the track as it descends with a wide stream on your right. Pass the remains of a dam to a gated bridge (Miners' Bridge).

6   Cross the bridge and the track to reach a path that turns left to run behind a stone wall. Take this path as it climbs steadily, with good views over Coniston village and the lake to the fells of Monk Coniston Moor.

7   When you meet a wall, follow it to cross a bridge, and pass through two gates to a stile. Cross the stile and turn right on a tarmac road, then round a right hand bend to climb to the fell gate just before the parking area. Take care along this stretch of road, which is very narrow.

13
Torver Back Common

An easy walk using woodland paths, lakeshore and moorland paths, that provides ample opportunity to linger by the lake or savour the views from the grassy mounds of Torver Common

Start: Layby on A593, near track junction. GR285945
Total distance: 8½km (5¼ miles)
Height gain: 250m (820 feet)
Difficulty: Easy; a few wet stretches and unbridged streams, finishing with a short section along a narrow busy road

1   From the layby walk along the road towards Coniston. Cross the bridge over Torver Beck and turn right through an iron wicket gate into a field. Go along the edge of the field, with a fence on your left, and heading for a gate. Continue ahead from the gate to cross two fences and a wall by step stiles and a gap.

2   Go half left (east) across a field to a gate giving access to a road. Cross the road to a signposted footpath, and use this for 150 metres/yards to Brackenbarrow Farm. There go over a stile on to a track enclosed by walls to continue through two gates to a wooded path (signposted: Torver Common).   Descend to a clearing on the shore of Coniston Water.

3   Turn right along the shore path, following it, first through woodland and then across open ground with steeply rising ground on your right. Keep going until your way is blocked by a wall. Bear right on an ascending path to a field gate, beyond which a track leads you to the road.

4   Turn right and follow the road, narrow in places and with no footpath, to the small village of Beckstones. Opposite the garage as you enter Beckstones, turn right into a small parking area to find a track on the left leading to a gate to Torver Common (signposted).

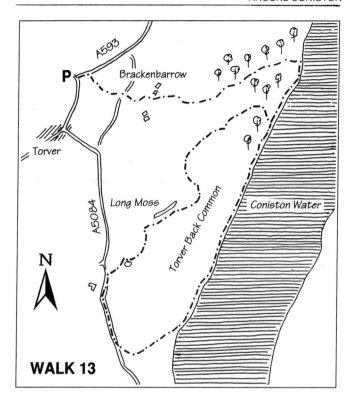

WALK 13

5   On the common, take the left hand track, which passes to the left of Kelly Hall Tarn, and stay with the track as it accompanies a wall to a col overlooking Long Moss Tarn. Turn right on a path beside Long Moss, and at its end turn left to step across the outflow and so gain an undulating path heading north, later descending through juniper bushes to a gate. Continue now to the lake shore on a path through oak woodland, and at the shore turn left to a small gate.

6   Walk on along a woodland path to the clearing encountered near the start of the walk, from where you can retrace your steps on a signposted woodland path, past Bracken Barrow to Torver.

14

Torver Low Common

An opportunity to get away from the crowds, over green paths and moorland used for centuries by the farmers of Torver for the grazing of sheep and cattle. The land is now owned by the national park.

Start: Layby on A5084. GR288927
Total distance: 8½km (5¼ miles)
Height gain: 230m (755 feet)
Difficulty: Easy; some wet spots and a few unbridged streams. Not advised in poor visibility

1 From the parking area cross the road and follow a signposted footpath through a gate, descending alongside a wall to cross Torver Beck by a wooden bridge. On a well-trodden path heading west, follow the course of Mire Beck for 600m/yds to a junction where you take the right hand fork to climb beside a tree-fringed gully to a small dam and reservoir.

2 From the dam take the path, right, first at the water's edge, but soon climbing to join a broad grassy track heading northeast. As you leave the reservoir behind the track descends, passing juniper bushes on the left, and then starts to climb to a grass-covered boulder. This boulder marks the start of a path going left (northwest), which you should follow. At first, as it crosses wet ground, it is indistinct, but improves as you go through heather to a stream and a path junction.

3 Cross the stream and take a clear path to the left through dry heather to a small tarn. Just before the tarn, go left to circle round its head, over a col, then left along the line of a wall descending to a lane. Turn left along the lane, and climb steadily to a gate. Keep along the lane until you reach a sign directing you left on a cement track to Greaves Ground Farm.

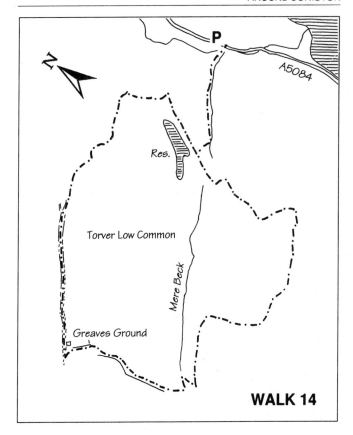

WALK 14

4   From the farm gate the route is waymarked by yellow arrows, left, then right, through three gates to a track running alongside a wall. Keep with the track through yet another gate, across a patch of wet ground, then past a small, and often dry, tarn. Here the track swings, right, into a field, but you require a path climbing to the left (south) beside the wall. When the wall turns away, keep with the path to a col and descend, and, keeping right at the next junction, head for a small group of birch trees and a stream crossing.

5   After the stream, turn left on a narrow path alongside the boggy

ground of Mere Moss to a small beck. Cross the beck to find a path running back to your right. Take this, back to the beck and a large yew tree, where the path turns to climb beside the beck in a shallow gully.

6   Near the top of the gully, the path climbs left to cross a col and descends between two small boulders on a green path through bracken.

7   At the end of the bracken follow its right hand edge round a small hill, then head for a solitary Scots pine, crossing a beck just before you reach the tree. Leave the tree, and pursue a clear path, first across a stream, and then round the base of a rocky outcrop to join a vehicle track heading northeast to a lane.

8   Turn left along the lane for 50m/yds to a signposted track on the left. Follow the track to the dam and reservoir visited earlier. Take the descending path, right, and follow it out to the Torver Beck bridge, and from there to the parking area.

Commons

Commons are areas of open land in England and Wales over which adjoining owners and occupiers have certain rights 'in common' with each other. Formerly, commons used to be the wastelands of medieval manors, and those enjoying rights over them - the 'commoners' - were invariably tenants of the lord of the manor.

The principal rights were pasturage, the right to graze cattle (known as pannage in the case of swine), piscary (the right to fish), turbary (the right to dig turf), and estovers (the right to take wood for repairs or firewood).

15

Miners' Tracks on Yewdale

This quiet walk follows green paths used by miners and quarrymen during the heyday of industrial activity among these southern fells of Lakeland.
Some of the tracks are now indistinct, and easy to miss, so be sure to chose a bright sunny day for a visit.
The splendid setting, amid gorse- and juniper-cloaked fellsides, must surely have lightened the burden of the hard-working quarrymen as they trudged wearily home at the end of their daily toil.

Start: Main car park, Coniston. GR303976
Total distance: 9km (5½ miles)
Height gain: 310m (1,015 feet)
Difficulty: Moderate; mainly on open, bracken-clad fellsides, but not advised in poor visibility

1   Leave the car park and turn left, going past the church to a road junction. Turn right along the main road for a few strides to a lane on the left beside the Black Bull Inn. Take this lane heading out of the village, and at the end of the surfaced section turn right over a stile on to a green path with a wall on the right.

2   Continue to a wooden gate, and there turn left on a narrow path climbing through bracken, gaining a little height to reach an oak tree. Take a moment to pause and admire the view over Coniston Water and the Yewdale Fells.

3   The way resumes by climbing through gorse bushes until the ground levels, joining a beck that leads you to a small tarn. Cross the beck at the tarn's outflow, and gain a little height to avoid wet ground. Look along the tarn for a cairn in a notch on the skyline, and head for it. From the cairn, your course is down the righthand side of a wet grassy gully to another cairn at its base. Cross the gully, left, on to an indistinct grassy path, and shortly descend, right, to cross a beck and circle left round wet ground, to climb a

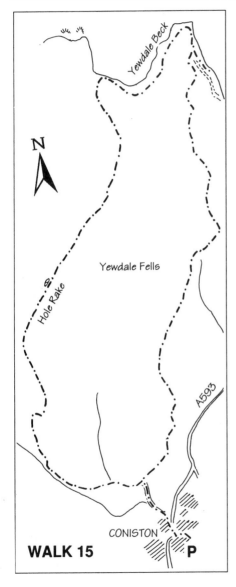

WALK 15

grassy gully with a cairn visible at the top. From this fine vantage point you look out over the boggy expanse of Yewdale Crag Moss, with the dark crags of Wetherlam looming in the distance. Descend into a shallow dip from which cairns mark the path to a grassy ledge.

4   Turn left on a high path to another cairn. Turn right, and of the three paths then available to you, take the faint one on the right to descend a broad grassy ramp through bracken — the other two paths climb to higher ground, so ignore them.

5   As you go down the path improves, with good views down the length of Yewdale and of Holme Fell across the valley. When you reach the head of a gill, the wet basin is circled left to gain a stone-edged

track directly opposite. Ignore the well-worn path, right, into the gill, as it leads to the abrupt headwall of a quarry. Descend the stone-edged path through bracken and juniper-clad crags to bend right, following a beck to a path on the left.

6   Turn left, cross the beck, and climb to a col, there passing through the remains of a wall. Now descend on a path flanked by bracken to a small quarry hut. Turn left to pass a larger building and a tunnel into underground workings. **Please note:** This mine is still worked, and is not a place to explore.

7   Staying with the main track, descend to the road. Turn left along the road for 200 metres/yards to Tilberthwaite car park, and on approaching the car park take an ascending path on the left (signposted).

8   Go past the entrances to Penny Rigg Slate Quarry and continue climbing to a path junction beside the ruins of a quarry hut. Fork left on a rising path (the course of a water race from Crook Beck to Penny Rigg Mine), and follow the rim of Tilberthwaite Gill.

9   The path narrows and is exposed as it navigates around a small rocky side-stream. Proceed with caution on the path following the line of a water race, and traverse above the gorge to a cairn at Crook Beck. Do not cross the beck, but turn left and follow its right bank on a cairned path. Cross a stream above a beautiful rowan-lined waterfall, and then climb steadily above the boggy wastes of Crook dam (now breached, but formerly supplying water to the Tilberthwaite workings below). Continue past a dangerous and flooded quarry to a small tarn at the head of the pass.

10 Cross the watershed and descend a dry grass gully, with the Old Man of Coniston directly ahead. The path bears left and descends in zigzags to the rear of a group of cottages (Irish Row). Keep left to the main track. Turn left along Church Beck, and follow the track to a bridge over the beck. Immediately below the bridge a magnificent waterfall hides an old mine. Go down the track, over a cattle grid to the surfaced road by which you can easily return to Coniston.

16

Coniston to Torver

This easy walk makes use of the trackbed of the former Furness railway, returning to Coniston on the high moorland packhorse trail of Walna Scar Road. The small village of Torver is ideally-placed for a refreshment halt.
Route-finding is clear throughout

Start: Main car park, Coniston. GR303976
Total distance: 9½km (6 miles)
Height gain: 260m (855 feet)
Difficulty: Easy/Moderate; take care on the descending narrow road from Walna Scar to Coniston station.

1   Leave the car park and turn left, going past the church, then cross the bridge to turn right on a road leading past the Sun Hotel. The road climbs and zigzags, and at a T-junction, turn left on a road passing small factory units and the Mountain Rescue Post. Keep on past a housing estate on the site of Coniston railway station. Follow the trackbed under the arch of a slate bridge and on to a gate spanning the track. Here a sign directs you to the road.

2   At the road, turn right, taking care against approaching traffic. After about 100m/yds, go left through a gate (signposted) on to a tree-lined track which leads down to the metalled access road to a caravan site. Keep going (southwest) along the road until it turns right. Here continue ahead on a track through trees to a wall blocking the track. At the wall turn left, through a gate, then by a grass track, keeping to the base of rising ground on your right. Bear right and follow the track across a beck to a ladder stile over a wall.

3   Over the stile, a grass track through trees leads you to a gate beyond which the track goes left across the top of a field. Keeping

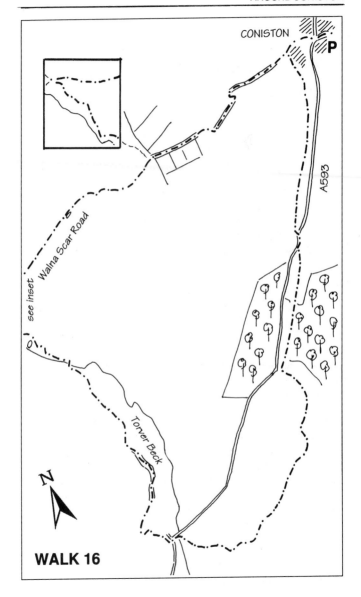

WALK 16

a hedge on your right, go past a gate and cattle grid to a field gate into the yard of Hoathwaite Farm.

4   Enter the yard and turn right at a signed opening between buildings to pass through sheep pens into a field, then keeping to the left hand fence to a step stile.

5   Cross the stile and follow a woodland path to a gap in a wall. Go through the gap, then head southwest across a field to a gate. The gate leads to a hedged track crossing four fields to a gated track at Bracken-barrow Farm. Through the gate turn right, go past the farm, then by another hedged track to the road. Cross the road to a step stile and head west across fields to the old railway track and a road.

6   Turn left along the road to a signposted bridleway on the right. If you wish to depart from the walk for a moment, you can go down to Torver for refreshments. Otherwise...

7   Turn right and follow a waymarked track through the village of Scar Head to join a walled bridleway. At the third gate, continue ahead across a bridge over Tranearth Beck on to a rough track leading to a gated sheep pen. Follow waymarks through the pen to a wooden bridge over Torver Beck, cross the bridge and turn left towards Bannishead Quarry.

8   Now follow the fence, right, to take an ascending terraced path beside the beck, heading for a large cairn on the Walna Scar Road. At the cairn, turn right, and descend between rock cuttings on a clear track heading northeast over open fellside, passing reed-filled Boo Tarn en route. The road runs down to a parking area on the right, and a gate at the top of a metalled roadway.
Go through the gate and, with care, follow the ensuing narrow road back to Coniston.